Hiraeth

Morgan Chavez

BookLeaf
Publishing

Presentation by *BookLeaf Publishing*

Web: www.bookleafpub.com

E-mail: info@bookleafpub.com

ISBN: 978-93-95087-63-6

First edition 2022

DEDICATION

To anyone who ever made me feel something big enough to write about, and to anyone who feels something when they read it- this is of you and for you.

ACKNOWLEDGEMENT

I don't know how to write something about everything that has helped me feel brave enough to put these words to paper without feeling like I've forgotten something critical. My heart is racing just thinking that one day I'll awake in a cold sweat and feel awful about not having mentioned a particular pen (Pilot G-2 07), but the deadline is nearing with alarming speed, so here we are.

Thank you to my mum, who read me bedtime stories and taught me how to write when I was jealous that my older sister got to learn how to in school, who bought me my typewriter, and who gave me a million worlds to plant my heart in over and over again.

Thank you to my sister, who loves me more than I deserve- always.

Thank you to my dad, who tried his best.

Thank you to Greg Delanty, my poetry professor and the first person to ever call me a poet. These words would never be seen by the world if he hadn't told me they matter.

Thank you to Frankie, who thought everything was beautiful.

Thank you to my sweet, adoring friends, who have read these poems a million times and who are the loves of my life.

To everyone and everywhere who has been a home to me- thank you, thank you, thank you.

PREFACE

To read when the skies are grey and when the cherry blossoms bloom.

hiraeth

i'm jealous of your tie
the way it hangs
around your neck,
just how i imagine i would
if you were mine.

jealous of that cup of coffee
as you wrap your hands around it,
familiarizing yourself
with its every curve;
jealous of the way
it warms you,
how you crave it
and press it
against your lips.

i'm jealous of the guitar
you reach for at 3 am
because you can't sleep
and it feels like home-
the way your fingers
trace delicately
across the strings,
how you've memorized
the luster

of its body,
smooth against
your ambling hands;
how you delight in
its resonant sound,
harmonizing beneath
the strum
of your touch.

but mostly i'm jealous of her
and the way your gaze
follows her every move
in that silk dress,
how the scent of her lingering
on your bedsheets drives you mad,
the way you adore her
with her chestnut hair
tucked behind her ear-
even when
she looks past you,
even when
i don't.

i'm jealous
of all the things
that get to have you,
and the one thing
you long to have.

frankie

you left
where everything was beautiful-
just the way
you viewed the world.
wherever your feet went,
your heart went,
growing flowers
on forgotten land.
the waters took you now,
but they will never put out your fire,
because a golden soul
always shines bright.

the gulf of alaska

i've heard that there is a place
where two oceans meet;
a dividing line in the center
i imagine my heart is that ocean
when i try not to love you:
gentle, cool blue
fighting dark, dark grey

staring at the wall

i didn't know
how much i desired
to be the space taken up
until you lay tired
with your head on my lap,
and my hands in your hair,
and the white noise of the tv
humming through the air,
and i thought that the shadow
in the shape of you and me
would look far too lonely
had you chosen another place to be

brooklyn

i felt the break in brooklyn
and we never stitched it up
you burrowed into me like the snow
and tore flesh when you left,
running me a fever
with your december heart.

i used to hang
onto the ways
you would avoid saying love
like they were special
like they belonged to us
like they were
beacons of hope
and not the cruelty
of your indifference.
it's amazing
how my heart grew used
to beating
in tune with your affection.
extraordinary how the organ heals,
scar tissue over scar tissue,
preparing for the next attack.

i remember being

wide-eyed
and innocent
because you hadn't yet
shown me
what it was to be spent.

you'd write me secret notes
on napkins
and i'd stuff them in my pocket
and you'd smile
when you saw me do it
out of the corner of your eye.

but there,
as we walked,
red lights reflected
on rainy pavement,
your face
had the candor
that your words
never did.

so i folded them up
and dropped them
into a stranger's garbage,
fighting the urge to look
over my shoulder to see
if you'd pick them up.

you were an actor
even in your sleep,
pulling me closer
and resting
your chin on my shoulder.
but even when we filled in
the space between our bodies,
there was a distance
which i
hungrily devoured
and which you
maintained
with fervor.

we were never made
for the city.
we weren't then
and we aren't now.
i wasn't made
for digging for change at tolls
and always
coming up short.
i wasn't made
for those shrieking sirens,
covering my ears and acting
like i didn't hear them all.
i wasn't made
to run around in the dark
hoping that we'd meet there.

i wasn't made
for your winter,
could never be home
to your ghost.

the woods

i remember
the look on your face
that came whenever i let myself
love you too much.
it took up
so much space in the room.
it was like you held something fragile
with no idea how to keep it
from falling apart.

i like to believe that you would have,
if you could,
instead of watching me fade
into that hollowed-out
version of me-
the version of me
that you knew
would eventually tire
of her hopeless hand
and fold.

i remember
when i gave you that ring
so you could match your mother
and i found it by your sink

six months later,
never worn,
just there.

and when i sent
messages at daybreak
only so that you might smile,
i'd wake,
opened but unreceived,
and you,
with hesitation on your fingertips.

sometimes, you loved me too.

other times your hand
would go limp in mine,
as if holding me meant
that there were promises
you had to keep.

i don't make myself sick
keeping track of you anymore.
i barely turn my head
to check
if your car is parked
at work when i drive by.
i refuse to bring pen to the pages
of the journal whose lines
were once filled with you.

there came a time when telling
the same underwhelming
love story
became too pathetic
for even a hopeless romantic like me.

but sometimes
i think of that face,
that how-do-i-get-her-to-stop-loving-me face,
and i slink back into myself
like you're there
in front of me
again.

i couldn't keep whispering my love for you,
hoping you wouldn't hear,
wishing you would.
my love was something
to warm you,
something you should
zip up to your chin,
and wear so much
that the elbows get thin
and the collar gets dirty.
it's not something
you reach for in the cold
and shrug off your shoulders
when it melts that away.
it's not something

that you keep packed away
and forget
that you own.

a.

i can't believe
he has the confidence
to smile when i run into him
in the frozen food aisle
of the market;
say that the sun
had made my skin pink,
suggest that we catch up
over pancakes.

did he feel me wince
when he hugged me?
a once familiar touch
drawing goosebumps to my skin.

i blamed it on the cold.
i suppose in part it was.

i've learned that he feels
he can call
after leaving my words
suspended in space--
how bitterly unfair of him
to assume we're still the same
when thoughts of him conjure

images of
lonely hotel beds
and record needles stuck
on the blood bank ep,
untouched plates of food,
me aching over the phone.

he acts like he
never kept me waiting,
pretends i'm the one that ran
when i moved myself to london,
got a new number,
stopped calling.
does he remember last october,
when pieces of us fell like autumn leaves,
one by one,
until the ground was covered in red?

i can't stand it that i loved him.
i can't stand it that i smiled back.

morning light

maybe it's the comfort i feel
with his body on mine,
or maybe it's the way the morning light
comes in and rests on everything,
touching whatever it can get
it's celestial hands on;

my cheek,
flushed from the night before
and pointed toward the window.

his kisses,
still glowing on my skin
like summer rain on pavement.

his tanned arm poking through
the space where my rib cage
dives in to meet my hips
and create the outline of my curves.

his fingers wrapping delicately
around my cold wrist,
thumb pacing the floor
of my skin in his sleep.

our clothes, discarded at the side of the bed,
still dripping with
the momentary trepidation
and the sudden surge of courage
that sent them flying
to land
haphazardly on hardwood.

the same hardwood
that our clumsy bare feet
stumbled on in complete darkness,
now illuminated with the kind
of soft light
that makes mornings feel infinite.

maybe it's the way
that the quiet feels more precious
when you don't want it to stir anything.
maybe it's all of that,
how it all feels soft as cotton.
maybe i don't know yet
exactly what it is,
but i like waking up next to him.

in one moment i knew
that every other love
had been designed to hurt,
and that his
never would.

standing in the park,
with the streaks of golden sun
pouring into the open
and landing
with intention onto his face,
i searched him for halos.

if there were others
in the world that day,
i didn't see them.

the lines of his face
are a daydream's frame,
his features in brushstrokes
so delicate
they could hang
on a gallery wall.

there is so much to behold

in his tight-lipped smile,
in his eyes illuminated in a hue
resembling that of
a dark cherry wood,
in the place where his hair
begins to grow
in such a particular fashion
that it can be so gracefully tucked
behind the curve of his ear.

i wondered if i touched him
if he would disappear-
a person so genuine,
a love so pure,
that it would never
send daggers
into my skin
or fill my lungs
with ash from the embers
of words i didn't say
burning on my tongue.

i wondered if i touched him
if it might stop my fingertips
from aching with desire.

august

friendship feels like
discarded aluminum cans
at the base of a waterfall
scrapes on your knees
from where you were pulled
up the rocks & into a hug
a towel slung over the railing,
drying in the sun
four forks in a bowl of pasta salad
watermelon juice
dripping down your arms
a deck of cards on the tabletop
the flash of a disposable camera
marking that moment in forever
pong balls bouncing off the ledge and rolling
down,
down,
down
cheeks red from laughter
and freckled from the sun
barefoot dances on barstools
a sleepy head on your lap
as moonlight creeps across the hardwood
the sound of early risers making pancakes
floating into your bedroom

wild flowers plucked
from the side of the road
and arranged delicately in a glass cup;
a breakfast table amenity
shaking awake boys in bunk beds
because breakfast's getting cold
the sweet sickness of the morning after
you passed out on an armchair
knowing there was safety
in the chaos around you

frankie ii

i try to chase away the realization
that i've spent more of my life
mourning the loss of your light
than i ever got to spend
watching the shine spill out of you.

on days like this i search for you
in the sky and in the breeze,
standing on top of the world,
watching the water pour down in a way
that reminds me of your grace.

i look for frankie feelings.

like seeing light
break through the clouds
or watching the sun
set over water.

like hearing "chocolate" in the car
or seeing christmas lights
in new york city.

like the warmth i feel
when i pull on your sweater,

the one you gave me
when you hardly even knew me
simply because i found it cozy.

like laughing with our best friend
and feeling you in the silence,
knowing we're strung together in infinity
because hearts that love
the same people always are.

you never left.
i've said it before.
we see dying starlight
in the skies of our atmosphere
long after it fades to black,
so why would it not
be the same for you?

phantom heartbreak

longing is
a nocturnal thing
that stands in the corner
of my room.

it stares at me
until i open my eyes
and tempts me
to lift my shirt
up to my nose
and inhale,
deeply,
so that it fills my lungs,
so that every molecule
of what i breathe is you-
the scent that lingers
because of the way
you were pressed up against me
the last time i wore it.

it turns me into
a writer in the dark,
insomniac eyes in my head,
hunched over a letter
frantically addressed

to you.

"i love you, i love you, why are you so far
away?"

feigning desire,
it sings
a sickly-sweet lullaby;
a choir of angels and devils
making midnight music
of your name.

the canyon

pink skies over the canyon.

in the moment when
the hot and stifling air of the day
begins to dissipate into breezes
that blow the sea-salted hairs
that escaped your bun
to tickle the nape of your neck,
i like to sit and watch the people,
the sweat dripping down
the back of my legs
turning balmy and cool with the night.

cradling my chin
in the palms of my hands,
i think of the way
i traced footsteps over streets,
think of the way
the iced chai tasted
after long hours of breathing in
beachwood dust,
press my fingertips lightly
to my pink, freckled cheeks
and smile at the brilliance of it all.

suddenly i don't feel
the rocks jutting into my back
or the dirt settling on my sticky skin,
and like a seashell pressed to my ear,
my mind echoes the ocean's droning lullabye,
a siren song pulling me
into a deeper calm.

gloucester road

every spring i think of you
and the way you were brand new to me
and how you remained lovely in my mind
like the cherry blossom trees
that i never had to see reach a winter.

you might be my favorite obsession,
with your petals preserved in time
unaffected by its ability
to turn things grey in its passage.

the sweet anticipation of you-
my hands flexing
in the dark forest of your curls,
your bright eyes and boyish smile
breaking through the dark,
warm caresses under covers,
soft cheeks,
peach and dimpled,
drawing me closer
to your face,
and a laugh-
its cadence of rhythmic punches
tantalizing enough to make
an atrophied heart

start pumping in quick bursts.

beautiful boy,
gilded in golden reverence,
you belong in the museum wing
where they keep precious things-
jewels and fading paints and gods of stone-
where i can see you every day,
gleaming with life,
the way you did
when the streets were lined
with brilliant, blooming color.

2022

firsts always feel
so romantic.
even as nostalgic as i am,
i've always loved
the newness of it all.

like new year's day
or the first page of a journal,
i rejoice at the notion
of crossing some
invisible threshold-
to cast yesterday
and all the yesterdays
off of me
as i brave the shores
of someplace other.

i used to take pause
at the risk that i might
someday miss that space
and wish i had stayed in it,
used to fear that i would lose it
to the constant tick of time-
people, moments, places,
swept from reality

and locked into dreams.

but how could distance
make them any less part of me
when from miles away,
i still feel love
in the very room i stand in,
when years pass from a moment
that is still all over me,
within me,
spilling out of me
and touching
all the new ground
i stand on?

the frost

this morning
when i stepped outside
into the winter air,
tinged with that
bruise-colored light
that blankets everything,
that snuffs out the noise
and makes you
tip-toe to your car
so as not to wake the day,
i felt impaled
by the stillness.

and while i sat in wait
for the world
to catch up to me
i saw in my windshield
a mirror
of my heart-
the way the ice cracks
in jagged patterns,
splintering,
delicate,
pulling apart
wherever it's met

with warmth.

i wanted to thaw it out,
to breathe my dewy breath
onto its impenetrable surface
and rub away
the iced-out armor.

but i was running late,
so i just drove
through the blur of it,
peeking through the spots
where the light came in.

for gods of love and war

i want to scream
and shatter glass,
send ripples
across the water,
be the reason the leaves
drop
from their branches.

i want to jolt
our world
from its four-year slumber
and when you'd wake,
you'd follow me
right to the cliff's
very edge.

and the earth
would fall
out from under us
and we'd reach
for each other
in the free fall,
touch hand
to trembling hand,
and let nature

send us spinning
to the place
we were meant
to land.

what i've been told

guys don't like it
when girls look fake.
a stay-at-home mom
isn't a career.
you only deserve
some of what I make.
cover up
when men are near.
you can get all you want
with just a pretty face.
i bet you don't
even understand football.
girls say no
because they like the chase.
your dress was pretty short,
after all.
you're far too serious,
why don't you smile?
my girlfriend
doesn't have to know.
you should go on
a diet for a while.
you don't look ladylike
when your bra straps show.
i hear it all the time,

so i thought i'd give it a whirl.
after all, i am pretty smart
...for a girl.

voir tout en rose

the idea of indulgence
is rooted in the temporary-
that dessert you buy
to feel local whilst on vacation,
those flowers from a street stand
you buy on your way home from work,
the fancy perfume
you spritz on in the morning,
the impossibly expensive tickets
you save up for-
your favorite artist
in your favorite city-
you know it won't last,
but you cherish it nonetheless.

you're the taste of tart raspberry
and rich chocolate on my tongue,
the feeling of velvety petals
on my fingertips,
the scent i drown myself in
when i wake,
the comforting melody
that breaks through
my atmosphere-
i love you for the way

you rush the floodgates of my senses;
even though i know you're fleeting,
i love you
for the way you fill my world up
while you are here.

five years

every revolution of the clock
is one that takes me
further from you.
days spiral on.
sometimes i look at the time
and it feels as though
its reached out its hands
and grabbed me by the throat,
my inescapable breath
trapped behind my teeth
at the thought of one year
without you.
two.
three.
four.
five.
it unforgivingly sweeps me in a current
to a place where you no longer exist,
too quickly
for me to catch my breath.
it's useless to swim against the tide.

other times it's unbearably, menacingly slow.

i think of my life

in two phases now.
in between the two
stands a green front door,
the life swirling around on one side
completely separate
to the one on the other.
behind the door sits a mother and daughter
reclined on the couch,
sipping ginger ale
and laughing at the tv.
an eternal reverie.
in front of it stands
a man i've never known,
a man in black slacks
and shiny shoes,
a man whose eyes grew anxious,
whose voice became muted
when he saw the recipient
of the message
he was sent to deliver.
a man here to tell me
that my father was dead.

that, i think,
is the slowest time
has ever felt.
everything happening
in the world around me
happened

in a sedated pace.
sounds were muffled
and light traveled
in streaks across the room
lingering like the trails
planes leave in the sky.
it passed by me like cars
on a midnight highway.
i don't remember moving
from that spot
to my bed,
i don't remember
how long i stayed there.
the dark took away
my perception of day and night.

light crashed back in
on the day I had to surrender you.
i traded in the grey
for a white dress and red roses.
i saw the color
of the sky.
the sun taunted me with the idea
that maybe I could bury
the hurt with you.
but instead
you,
along with all the feelings
i was trying to keep down,

were ignited in flames.
bowing my head on the box,
i wanted to rip you out of there,
to shake you awake.
it all came out
in silent sobs
that left damp spots
on the unpolished wood.
part of me
went in there with you.

this pain
was different.
it was my chest tightening
when my mum cried
to your song on the radio.
it was squeezing my eyes shut
when my sister got home
so i didn't have to see
her face
when she heard the news.
it was me pulling out
the letters you wrote me
so many times that the pages
eroded at the creases,
me thumbing through
the yellow notepad paper
trying to will you
back to life with your words.

it was me slinking up the stairs
with seven old photographs
and the knowledge that those
were the last ones
that you would be in.
it was,
in no chronological order,
sadness,
fear,
guilt,
love,
regret,
nostalgia,
anger,
confusion.

time,
i learned,
has no predictable route.

still,
memories of us are folded
into the pockets of my mind.
intricately,
like how a baker kneads flour
into dough.
like when it rains
and i see you
clomping up the stairs,

chasing three-year-old me
into a little tent
in my pajamaed feet,
mocking the monster
from my favorite storybook.
i always giggled,
but you always pretended
you couldn't hear me.
you were my giant,
and i wasn't scared.

and that was how time took me
for a while,
just like that,
like a supercut
of the moments
that would never be enough.
my relationship to you
in a constant
state of flux.

these past five years
i've counted time
with different measures.
i've measured it in sunsets
i took the time to watch,
drinks cheersed
with people i love,
steps i've taken

on new streets,
words i've spoken
instead of holding in.
i've measured it
in cups of tea,
in good nights' sleeps,
in photos on glossy sheets
hung haphazardly
on the wall.
i've measured it in genuine laughs
and desperate cries,
in moments that make
my cheeks turn pink
and my heart beat fast.
i let life pass in that way
because that's how
you'd like it to be-
me in awe of everything,
enchanted by each moment
that i'm here
when you can't be,
with maybe
just the remnants
of little girl
missing her daddy-
and i promise
i'll keep counting
time like this,
in a million tiny moments,

a million tiny stories
to tell you in the end.

you are your home

it's always been so easy for me
to get swept up
in the idea of running,
my incendiary heart abound
for somewhere that felt like home.
when the city i loved began to look
like empty streets with dead-ends,
i placed my finger on the globe
and spun.
my lust for newness
was the most comforting sin,
preventing me from wanting anything
enough to stay.

this morning i woke up
in a new city,
thinking about a man
i didn't know last year,
and stood facing
myself in the mirror,
wondering
if i'm doing it all wrong.
but the sight of me
sobered me,
as i turned to the side

and saw the black ink
etched onto my ribcage
as a reminder of what
i didn't always believe,
what i've lived enough to learn-
you can run from place to place.
you can find residence in
as many people as your soul encounters,
and then run from them, too.
but you can't run from you.
if home exists anywhere,
it's exactly where you stand,
for you are your home.